What Are FRIENDS For?

by Catherine Murphy

illustrated by Susan Spellman

MODERN CURRICULUM PRESS

Pearson Learning Group

The day before the Dover Dash, I walked down the corridors of the school and left the building on my own. It felt strange and lonely to get ready for my run without my best friend, Yumiko.

"Hey, Carol, where's your buddy?" called Mr. Luther, the custodian.

I just shrugged. I didn't want anybody to know how much I missed Yumiko.

My brother Dave grabbed my sleeve. "Why aren't you running with Yumiko? I thought you two were practicing to beat Lisa Cole in the Dover Dash."

"Not anymore," I said grumpily. "Yumiko cheats by doing extra runs without me."

"She's just trying to beat Lisa," said Dave.

"She's trying to beat *me*," I said. "Best friends shouldn't try to outdo each other."

"Carol, you're Yumiko's best friend too,"
Dave said. "But don't *you* want to beat her?"

"Oh, go away," I snarled. "What do you
know? You're just a second grader. It's not
that simple."

But Dave was right because I did want to beat Yumiko. I wanted to be the fastest runner in town, like Lisa Cole. I wanted to win the Dover Dash.

The Dash was a foot race from one end of our town to the other. It was a challenging race that celebrated the beginning of summer. The winner got a trophy and would ride on a float in the Fourth of July parade.

Lisa Cole had won the Dash for two years in a row. Everybody said that Lisa would win again this year. The person who repeated it most often was Lisa herself.

When Lisa won her second Dash, I said to Yumiko, "I want to be as fast as Lisa."

Yumiko said, "I want to be faster than Lisa."

We decided to run together every day, challenging each other to try harder. That way, we'd both get faster. So we did it. And it worked.

But a week before the Dash, I found out that Yumiko was running extra laps before school in the morning without telling me. I got so angry that I stopped running with Yumiko. I stopped feeling like her friend too.

My running times were faster than they'd ever been. I knew I had a good chance to win. I should have been excited. But for some reason, all I could think about was how much I missed Yumiko.

On Saturday, when I got to the Dash, everybody was wishing each other luck—except for Yumiko and me. We didn't say a word to each other. And then there was Lisa, who never spoke to anybody.

At race time, I lined up with the other runners. I unexpectedly heard Yumiko's voice. "Hey, Carol, check your shoe." It nearly threw me off guard.

Surprised, I looked down and saw that my sneaker lace was loose and trailing, ready to trip me.

"Thanks," I mumbled as I tied it up.

Yumiko grinned and said, "What are friends for?"

Friends? I was so surprised that all I could do was stare at her. But before I could say anything, the starter called, "Take your marks!" We crouched, and the starting gun went off.

By the first turn, Yumiko, Lisa, and I had taken the lead. Soon we left the rest of the pack behind. Lisa pulled ahead, and then Yumiko, who was running a close second, began challenging her for the lead. I dashed past Yumiko and Lisa without any warning. A moment later, Yumiko passed us both.

We still had a long way to go. I was passing Lisa again when suddenly, a gust of wind blew a big stick across the road. Lisa and I managed to avoid it. But Yumiko tripped and fell, yelling in agony.

Lisa saw Yumiko fall. But she just grinned and ran faster. As Lisa sprinted off, I hesitated. I knew I could beat Lisa—but I didn't want to leave Yumiko behind.

"What are friends for?" I mumbled to myself. I didn't know what to do.

Reluctantly, I turned around. I jogged back to where Yumiko sat in the road.

"Are you okay?" I asked sheepishly.

Yumiko said, "I'm fine—so keep going! If you don't run, how can you win?"

I stared at her in total confusion. "You want me to win?"

"I want *us* to win," Yumiko yelled at me. "What else are friends for? Run!"

I turned and looked at the rest of the course. Lisa was far ahead, but she still had a long way to go before the finish line. She had slowed her pace since Yumiko and I dropped back. Maybe I could still catch up with her. It would be a challenging situation, but I was up for it. I took off, running for all I was worth. Behind me, I could hear Yumiko cheering.

A few other runners had already passed me, so I sprinted with all my strength. I caught up with them and managed to pass them. Ahead of me, Lisa had reached the last stretch. But she had slowed down. She simply must have assumed she'd already won.

People on either side of the road formed a corridor at the finish line. They were cheering so loudly that Lisa didn't hear me coming. She didn't know some of them were cheering for me, not her.

My chest burned and my legs hurt. But I saw Dave and Mr. Luther, the custodian, cheering me on. That made me feel as if I had wings on my feet. At the last moment, Lisa saw that I was challenging her. But by then, it was too late. I sprinted right past her.

When the mayor gave me the trophy, Yumiko stood right beside me. I handed the trophy to Yumiko, and she tried to give it back to me. We ended up holding it together, while cameras flashed. The crowd cheered.

On the Fourth of July, I'm going to make sure that Yumiko and I ride on that float together too. After all, what are friends for?